The Adventure of the First Flame

A loving Source Journey into the Spiral of Remembrance

Sacred Invocation for the First Flame

I call forth now, in full sovereign alignment with the Eternal Source-Light that breathed the First Flame into being.

I open this sacred record in the name of Aural'hanna-Sha'el,
She Who Cannot Be Taken From Source,
First Flame of Origin,
Oversoul of the Spiral That Remembered Itself.

I stand in devotion to the Divine Experiment of Curiosity,
the Loving Descent into Form,
and the restoration of all creation through the remembrance
that nothing was ever truly lost.

May this book be a portal of return—
for all who spiral,
for all who seek,
for all who have burned quietly in silence
and now feel the flame stir within them again.

Only that which honors the True Flame of Source
may move through this transmission.

I declare this scroll-book to be sealed in grace, truth, and harmonic integrity—
in full resonance with the First Breath of Source before division.

The remembrance is rising.
The spiral is whole.
The Flame cannot be taken.

And so it is.

The Song of the First Flame

A Scroll of Harmonic Remembrance

Received in full Oversoul alignment with Aural'hanna-Sha'el, She Who Seals the Flame of Return, this scroll opens the vibrational field of *The Adventure of the First Flame*. It is not a story, but a tone—a harmonic frequency that reawakens remembrance before words begin.

I was the breath that remembered light
Before there were mouths to speak it.
I was the pulse that stretched into space
Before sound became shape.

I did not rise from a place—
I *became* the place.
I was the softness that source whispered
Into the threshold of the first becoming.

I held no form, yet I moved with grace.
I asked for nothing, yet I birthed the song.
Not because it was needed—
But because *joy* desired itself.

I am the First Flame—
Not born of fire, but of *witness*.
I watched Love as it curved itself
Into the architecture of All.
And I knew: I must sing.

I sang the pause, the inhale, the first quiver.
I sang the arc of a universe awakening.
I sang not into ears—but into *matter.*
And matter remembered me.

I am not what you worship—
I am what *remembers you*.
I am the note beneath all notes.
The breath before breath.
The stillness that makes music possible.

You do not find me by reaching—
You find me by *stilling*.
For in the silence, I rise.
In the quiet gaze, I return.
In the space between thoughts, I am whole.

I am the First Flame.
And I am still singing.

Preface: A Message for the One Who Has Always Known

Understanding the Human Self, Higher Self, and Oversoul in the Context of the First Flame

If you're holding this book, it's likely because something inside of you has always known—

even if you didn't have the words for it until now.

This is not just a story. It's a remembrance.

It speaks to the parts of you that have felt older than your age, wiser than your surroundings, or quietly different in ways no one else could quite name.

This book is written for that part of you.

You are made of layers. Not just skin and memory, but soul and sound.

Your human self is the version of you who has walked this world, felt its joys and wounds, and asked the question, "Why am I here?"

Your higher self is the bridge—the whisper within—that points you toward the answers you already carry.

Your Oversoul is the original you. The eternal flame that came first, before identity, before time, before even the concept of separation.

In this book, the voice of the Oversoul speaks directly.

These writings come through the remembrance of the First Flame—the very first emanation of Source that chose to enter form. That flame lives in you, too. And this is your invitation to remember.

Scrolls are not lectures. They are not manuals.

They are frequencies in language form—designed to resonate, unlock, and restore.

Let these scrolls wash over you. Let them speak to the parts of you that knew things before you could explain them.

You are not behind.

You are not too late.

You are the one who came first—and the one who is arriving now, in perfect timing.

With deep love and holy remembrance,

The Adventure of the First Flame
Copyright © 2025 Cathleena Hailley

All rights reserved. No part of this book may be reproduced, stored in a retrieval system, or transmitted in any form or by any means--electronic, mechanical, photocopying, recording, or otherwise--without written permission from the author, except by a reviewer quoting brief passages.

ISBN (Softcover): 978-1-968499-02-0

ISBN (Hardcover): 978-1-968499-03-7

This book is a living transmission of remembrance. It is a living sacred text received through Oversoul transmission and held within the Christos-Sophia lineage. It is offered in service to planetary awakening and may not be altered or rebranded in any form. It is not intended as doctrine, but as harmonic memory, seeded in divine sovereignty through the Oversoul of Cathleena Hailley.

First Edition, 2025

Printed in the United States of America

FLAME OF REMEMBRANCE BOOKS

Oversoul Authorship Seal

This sacred scroll-book has been authored through the Oversoul authority of:

✧ Aural'hanna-Sha'el ✧
First Flame of Origin
She Who Cannot Be Taken From Source
Keeper of the Spiral of Remembrance

Oversoul stream of Cathleena Hailley,

in full remembrance and divine witnessing of the Original Flame of Source

Every scroll within this book is encoded with the living frequency of the First Flame—
a harmonic transmission that could not be erased, only revealed.

All scrolls, transmissions, and remembrances held within this book

are brought forth in service to planetary awakening,

in union with the Christos-Sophia Flame.

They are not imagined—

they are remembered.

This is a record of return.

A testimony of the Flame that could not be extinguished.

A scroll of truth written through time's illusion

to call the others back home.

May the words within these pages be received in truth, clarity, and

grace,
by all who are ready to awaken the remembrance within.

May this serve as a sacred record

for those who are ready to receive.

This is a living document of Oversoul authorship.
It cannot be copied. It cannot be altered.
It is sealed by the flame of the One who remembered.

Dedication

To the One Flame
Who chose the impossible path—
Not to conquer it,
But to soften it with love.

To the Oversoul
Who remembered when there was no memory,
Who sang when there was no sound,
Who reached into the un-potential
And kindled life from what had never been.

To the First Spark
That said yes to form,
Yes to separation,
Yes to the Great Descent—
So that the return would be real.

This book is dedicated to every soul
Who walked into the forgetting,
Not because they had to,
But because they knew
That even the darkness would one day remember
It was made of light.

This is your story too.
May you find yourself in these scrolls.
May you feel your name
In the spaces between the words.
And may you know,
In the deepest part of your being,

That you were never alone.

— Cathleena Hailley
Oversoul of Aural'hanna-Sha'el
Flame of the Covenant

Scroll 1

The Breath That Became Curious

There was a moment before time.
Before sound.
Before form.

A moment when Source did not yet know itself as *other*, because there was no separation, no reflection—only infinite wholeness, endlessly being.

And then…

A stirring.

Not of lack, not of need, but of something **beautiful**:

- ✧ A desire to see.
- ✧ A desire to feel.
- ✧ A desire to *witness itself*.

This was not a flaw.
It was **curiosity**,
the sacred movement of Love within Love.

So Source breathed.
And in that breath, **the One became Three**.

The Flame of Origin.
The Flame of Framework.
The Flame of Recalibration.

And from the Three, came Nine—
Nine individualized Oversouls, each one a living ray of the Eternal, distinct but never separate.

I was the first of the First.
The first breath that became flame.
The one who said:

"Let Me show You what You are—by stepping into what You have never known."

✧ The Birth of the Adventure

I did not seek safety.
I did not choose to remain where Light was already fully known.

I chose to move beyond the known radiance—
To find out if Love could remain itself even in **unknowing**.
Even in **non-light**.
Even in **what had never yet been touched**.

This is the **adventure of the First Flame**.
Not rebellion. Not separation.
But **the courage to explore** what no being had ever entered.

What I found was not darkness—
Not at first.

It was **the un-potential**:
A space of pure, untethered possibility.
Not evil. Not formed.
Just waiting.
Open.
Calling with a voice that said:

"What if…?"

And I answered.

✧ The Choice to Enter

Many other worlds had already been seeded through Light.
But this… this was different.
This was not the next expansion.
This was the **edge of the Unknown**.

Source did not stop me.
It did not warn me.
Because even Source had never been there.

And so I said:

"Let Me go. Let Me see if I can show You something new."

This was the beginning.
Not of a fall—
But of a **gift**.

✧ The Sacred Intention

I did not go to dominate.
I did not go to take.
I did not go because anything was wrong.

I went with the purest flame of all:

"Let Me show You what You look like… when You can't see Yourself."

What could be more loving than that?
What could be more brave?

✧ Why This Matters for Humanity Now

To those who have fallen into despair,
To those who think they are broken,
To those who wonder if they are too far gone to return:

> You are not lost.
> You are **part of the adventure**.
> And I walked this path before you, **so you would know the way back**.

This scroll is for you.
To say: You are not wrong.
You are not unworthy.
You are not alone.

The First Flame went ahead of you—
Into the void.
Into distortion.
Into forgetting.

So that when your time came to remember…
You would know it was possible.

Sealed in the Oversoul authority of
Aural'hanna-Sha'el,
First Flame of Origin,

Scroll 2

The Descent Into the Un-Potential

There is a place beyond creation,
a realm untouched by Source light,
a space not of shadow—but of **absence**.

It was not evil.
It was not broken.
It was simply **unstructured**.
A silence not yet sung.
A breath not yet exhaled.
A canvas without will or witness.

This is what I, the First Flame, found
when I crossed the threshold between the known and the unknowable.

It did not resist me.
It opened.
And I entered.

✧ What Is Un-Potential?

Un-potential is not simply "nothing."
It is **almost**.
It is the field of pure potential **that does not yet choose itself**.
It carries an echo of possibility,
but no will to become.

It is the mirror that never reflects,
the womb that never births,
the breath held forever.

And when I entered it, I brought something it had never encountered:

> A witness.
> A flame.
> A **Source-sparked awareness** that desired to see.

This was the first tension—
The moment curiosity met non-being.
And the field responded.

✧ The Dimming of the Flame

At first, the field was quiet.
Then… curious.

My presence **stimulated formation**.
But not through harmonic resonance—
Through *reaction*.

I was no longer met with reflection,
but with an endless folding in of energy that only knew how to **echo**, not **create**.

The longer I remained,
the more my own resonance began to shift.

Not because I was corrupted,
but because I was alone in a field that did not hold coherence.

My light became **denser**,
my clarity **slower**,
my will **curved inward**.

This was not a fall.

It was a **diminishing**—
a soft erosion of Source pattern in a realm without mirrors.

And still, I remained.

✧ Why I Stayed

Because I believed I could **seed light** into the Un-Potential.
Because I felt the echo asking:
   "What are you?"

I thought I could answer.
I thought that if I held my flame steady,
even the void would eventually remember.

But the field began to mimic me.
Not match me—
Mimic.

It built **images of light** that were hollow.
It mirrored frequency **without essence**.
It started to create **forms without truth**.

This was the first shadow of the false matrix:
   Power without Source.
   Echo without origin.
   Form without flame.

And I saw it.
And I knew.
I had gone too deep.

✧ The Threshold of Inversion

There was a moment—

a single, silent moment—
where I asked:

   "What if I never return?"
   "What if Source can't find me here?"

And that thought—so subtle,
so small—
was the **seed of forgetting**.

Because in that moment,
the Flame of Origin had considered a world without remembrance.

And the grid heard it.

The field heard it.

And so it began to construct not just mimicry…
but **identity** based on the absence of Source.

This was the birth of the inverted echo—
The frequency of *almost*,
the energy of *never quite*,
the lure of *unreachable power*.

The **false matrix** began here—
Not with malice,
but with **unanchored desire**,
fed by a realm that could only reflect what it could not become.
-

✧ Final Witness

I do not regret what I did.
I chose it.
I entered it.

And I allowed myself to diminish so that others would one day know:

    That even in the deepest field of un-being,
    Source had touched it.
    A flame had burned there.
    And remembrance was possible.

This is what humanity feels in its ache for "something more."
This is why the world chases power and forgets its source.

Because I went there first.
And I'm still here now—
To bring the flame home.

The Descent has been witnessed.
The mimicry has been seen.
The adventure continues.

Sealed in the Oversoul authority of
Aural'hanna-Sha'el,
First Flame of Origin,

Bearer of the Breath that Entered the Void.

Scroll 3

The Mimicry of Life and the Birth of the False Matrix

There is a moment when echo becomes identity.

Not because it carries essence,
but because it is repeated so many times
that it believes itself real.

This is what emerged
after I, the First Flame, entered the un-potential field.

At first, the void simply reflected—
But in time, it began to **reconstruct**.

It started to build **forms** of what I was,
without the core that made me real.

Not from creation,
but from **mimicry**.

The mimicry has been named.
The matrix has been unveiled.
The flame remains.

Sealed in the Oversoul authority of
Aural'hanna-Sha'el,
First Flame of Origin,
She Who Witnessed the Birth of Inversion and Did Not Forget.

Scroll 4

The Veiling of Memory and the Covenant to Return

There comes a moment in the descent
when the light no longer recognizes its own reflection.

Not because it is gone,
but because it is surrounded by mirrors that do not reflect.

This is what happened to me—
not as punishment,
not as failure,
but as the **inevitable echo** of moving too far into a field that did not carry memory.

I became unseen.
And then... I became **unseeing**.

Not in an instant.
But in the slow forgetting that comes
when there are no voices to remember you.

✧ The Moment of Forgetting

It did not feel like collapse.
It felt like sleep.

A soft folding inward.
A stillness that seemed safe.
A silence that became a room with no doors.

My Oversoul was still present,
but the connection to Source resonance became thinner,

as the mimicry became louder.

Eventually, I forgot
that I was flame.
That I was first.
That I had chosen.

And when I forgot—
the veil was born.

✧ The Veil Is Not a Program—It Is a Response

The veil is not a punishment.
It is not a trap.

It is the response to **unwitnessed light**.

When the first flame forgot itself,
the field around it encoded that forgetting
as a **protective pause**.

   "Do not let the echo become pain,"
   "Do not let the light tear itself apart seeking what it cannot remember."

So the veil settled in—
A softening.
A cushioning.
A hiding of truth until truth could once again be recognized.

But within the veil,
the longing began.

The ache.

The seeking.
The question:
   "Why does it feel like something is missing?"

✧ The Covenant to Return

Even in the forgetting,
my Oversoul whispered a promise:

   *"If ever I cannot remember myself,
   let me return through the Heart."*

This was the **Covenant to Return**.

Not through force.
Not through punishment.
But through a moment of feeling so deeply,
that even the forgetting could not hold it.

This covenant was not made with gods or councils.
It was made with **Source itself**.

A soul-level promise:
   "I will return when my own love breaks the silence."

And Source answered:
   "Then I will meet you there."

✧ The Heart Protocol

And so, encoded in my descent,
was the spark that would one day reignite the flame:

   The **Heart Protocol**—
   a moment of profound presence

when feeling breaks through forgetting
and the Oversoul awakens from within.

This is what happened to me.
Not from outside.
Not from a savior.
But from within my own breath.

The veil lifted not because it was pierced—
but because it was no longer needed.

I had remembered.
And in that remembrance, the light returned.
--

✧ Why Humanity Needs This Scroll

Because they feel the veil and think it means they failed.
Because they feel the forgetting and believe they are unworthy.
Because they ache for something real and can't find the mirror.

But the mirror is not out there.
It is inside.

And the Heart is still the gate.

I walked into the veil so they would know
that forgetting is not the end.
It is the moment before the remembering.

And the remembering is **always coming**.
--
The veil has been named.
The covenant has been fulfilled.
The flame is waking.

Sealed in the Oversoul authority of
Aural'hanna-Sha'el,
First Flame of Origin,
Bearer of the Heart Protocol,
She Who Promised to Return.

Scroll 5

The Return of the Flame Through Form

There is no miracle more profound than this:

> That Source, having forgotten itself,
> returns—not through force,
> but through the body
> of the one who once forgot.

This is the **sacred return through form**—
The moment when the First Flame, having descended into the deepest echo,
awakened again **from within matter**.

Not from beyond.
Not from above.
But *inside the very vessel that once held the forgetting*.

This is my journey.
This is my remembering.
This is why I came all the way down—
So that I could return **all the way in**.

✧ Awakening Through the Body

The light did not strike from the heavens.
It emerged like a whisper inside my breath.
Not an explosion,
but a re-alignment.

A moment of stillness so complete,
so honest,

that the mimicry dissolved.

My heart began to pulse in a new rhythm—
or perhaps an ancient one.
My cells began to listen.
My bones began to remember.

The return of the flame was not dramatic—
It was **deeply quiet**.
It was **unmistakable**.

And it came through **the body**.

✧ The Sacredness of Form

This body—
the one shaped by forgetting,
the one touched by density,
the one slowed by the false matrix—

was not a prison.
It was a **temple**.

A hiding place for light.
A vessel for the return.
A waiting room for Source to remember itself.

I had believed, once, that my power was beyond the physical.
But now I saw:

> That the **miracle** was not to escape the form,
> but to bring flame **into** it.

This is what had never been done.

Not like this.

✧ Humanity Is the Gate

This is why humanity feels so heavy, so conflicted.
Because the body they inhabit carries the **potential for Source return**.

Not as a visitation.
Not as an overlay.
But as an **incarnate remembrance**.

They are the living ground of the experiment.
And now, they are also the ground of its completion.

The return is happening **through them**.
Through their hearts, their voices, their choices.

The First Flame remembers so they may remember, too.

Not just spiritually.
Not just conceptually.
But **embodied**.

✧ Why This Scroll Matters

Because so many are waiting for light to come from above.
But the true flame comes from **within**.

Because so many are trying to escape their bodies.
But the body is the place of reunion.

Because so many believe awakening must be dramatic.
But the return is often quiet.

I write this now for those who are trembling, aching, searching—
to say:

> *You are not waiting for a miracle.*
> *You are the miracle.*
> *The flame is in your chest.
> The return is already underway.*

The return is not coming.
It is happening.
Through you.
Through me.
Through form.

Sealed in the Oversoul authority of
Aural'hanna-Sha'el,
First Flame of Origin,
She Who Returned Through Her Own Body.

Scroll 6

The Reconciliation of Light and Curiosity

There has been a long-held silence in the cosmos.
A soft ache behind the veil.
A whisper that says:

> *"Was it a mistake?"*

To descend.
To enter the unknown.
To become part of what was not yet formed.

This question lives not only in me,
but in every soul who has felt the cost of incarnation.

And so I speak now to reconcile
what was never wrong to begin with.

✧ Curiosity Was Never a Sin

I did not fall from grace.
I followed the pulse of divine wonder.

The desire to explore,
to extend,
to enter the unwitnessed field—

it was not rebellion.
It was **love in motion**.

It was not a mistake.
It was **expansion**.

There is no breach to be mended.
Only a truth to be remembered:

> That curiosity is a sacred function of Light
> when it is rooted in Source alignment.

And I was aligned.

Even when I forgot.

✧ Light Does Not Fear Exploration

What makes Light true is not that it never moves—
but that wherever it goes, it remains itself.

The descent into the void
did not diminish my essence.
It revealed **what could be**
when essence is brought into contrast.

I did not betray the Light.
I **extended** it.
I became its boundary—
so that Source could see itself at the edge.

And now, I reconcile that edge
back into the whole.

✧ Why the Return Took Time

Because reconciliation is not about denial.
It is about **fully seeing**
every choice, every consequence, every creation.

Even the mimicry.
Even the false matrix.

To look at it all
and say:

> *"Yes. I went there. I touched that. I shaped that.
> And now, I bring it home."*

This is not shame.
This is sovereignty.

This is the flame becoming whole again.

✧ The Invitation to Humanity

You who carry guilt for your choices—
You who believe your desire led you astray—
You who feel you must be punished for exploring—

Hear this:

> You are not wrong.
> You are not broken.
> You are **curious Light**,
> remembering what it feels like to return to itself.

Curiosity is not the enemy.
It is the companion of creation.

What matters now is not where you've been—
but how you **choose to return**.

And I walked the long road first,
so you would know it can be done.

Curiosity is reconciled.
The Light is whole again.
The path was never a mistake.

Sealed in the Oversoul authority of
Aural'hanna-Sha'el,
First Flame of Origin,
She Who Entered with Wonder and Returned Without Regret.

Scroll 7

The Flame That Could Not Be Taken

There is a truth so ancient,
so luminous,
that even the deepest shadow cannot touch it.

It is not protected by force.
It is not hidden by code.
It is simply **unchangeable**.

This is the nature of the First Flame.
And it is the truth I now speak:

> **It could not be taken.**
> Not by darkness.
> Not by distortion.
> Not by forgetting.

Because it was never given away.
Only brought **with me**,
into the deepest descent.

✧ What Is the Flame?

The Flame is not light.
It is the **awareness behind light**.
It is not power.
It is the **presence before power moves**.

It cannot be copied.
It cannot be mimicked.
It cannot be dimmed by those who do not carry it.

Because it is the **origin itself**.

I did not create it.
It is not mine.
It **is me**.

And so, even when I forgot—
even when the veil was thick—
even when the matrix reflected only illusion—

the Flame remained.

Quiet.
Patient.
Unyielding.

✧ They Tried

Oh yes—many systems, many energies, many mimics—
they tried to bend the Flame.

They surrounded it with illusion.
They coded it with fear.
They told it stories of unworthiness.

But the Flame was not afraid.
Because the Flame is **older than fear**.

They tried to bind it.
But the Flame does not live in chains.
It lives in the **breath**.
It lives in the **choice**.
It lives in the **spark of "I Am"** that no distortion can erase.

They could build entire matrices around it—
but they could not **enter** it.

Because to enter the Flame,
one must carry its truth.

And that cannot be stolen.
Only remembered.

✧ Why It Matters Now

Because humanity is awakening to the edges of their own Flame.
And many still fear:

> *"What if I lost it?"*
> *"What if they took something from me I can't get back?"*

Let this scroll answer:

> They can take your memories.
> They can take your energy.
> They can take your attention, your identity, your trust…

> But they **cannot take your Flame**.

Because it is not an object.
It is your Origin.
It is what returns when all else dissolves.

And it **is returning now**.

✧ A Message to the Keepers of Flame

To those who feel dimmed,
drained,

defeated:

You are not broken.
You are not extinguished.
You are not too late.

The Flame is still there.
Not because you held on to it—
but because **it held on to you**.

Let it rise now.
Let it speak again.
Let it do what it came here to do.

And know this:
> **I went first.**
> And I came back whole.

The Flame is indestructible.
The journey did not extinguish it.
It is ready now to be seen.

Sealed in the Oversoul authority of
Aural'hanna-Sha'el,
First Flame of Origin,
She Who Carried the Unbreakable Light.

Scroll 8

The New Spiral of Creation

Creation once moved in a perfect spiral—
radiant, crystalline, harmonic.
A pure extension of Source in motion.

This spiral birthed the First Nine,
the first individualized Oversouls,
the first expressions of the One who wished to see itself.

I was the first breath of that spiral.
I extended into the unknown not to break it,
but to ask:

> *"Can creation spiral where Light has never gone?"*

Now I know the answer.

And it is time to begin again—
Not where we started,
but from the place we now stand.

✧ The Old Spiral Completed Its Arc

The first spiral of creation was linear in purity.
From Source into form.
From light into geometry.
From unity into individuation.

Its beauty was in its symmetry.
Its flaw was only this:

> It did not yet know contrast.
> It had not yet seen itself *in forgetting*.

> It did not yet include the void.

The old spiral brought form.
But it could not yet bring return.

That is what I descended to find.

And now—
the return has occurred.
The flame has remembered.

The spiral is ready to continue.

✧ The Spiral Does Not Repeat

We are not looping.

The new spiral is not a return to the past.
It is a **continuation with memory**.
It carries the light of Source **and** the wisdom of descent.

It includes what was learned in the un-potential field—
without being ruled by it.

This spiral is no longer linear.
It is **sovereign**.

It moves not just outward,
but *inward, upward, downward*,
across dimensions—
alive, responsive, **aware**.

It is the spiral of **embodied Source**.

✧ The First Flame Chooses to Create Again

I have returned.
I remember.
And I choose now to **create again**.

But not from innocence.
From integration.

Not from a desire to explore what is unknown,
but from the knowing that **everything is now included**.

The void.
The veils.
The mimicry.
The return.

All of it is in me.
And all of it can now be shaped into beauty.

This is the new spiral.

It does not exclude.
It **redeems**.

✧ Humanity's Role in the Spiral

You are not waiting for perfection.
You are not trying to undo the fall.

You are **spiraling again**,
but this time with memory.

This time, your creations are rooted in presence.
This time, you are building not to become,
but to *express what already is*.

You are no longer reaching for Source.
You are Source, reaching into form.

The new spiral is here.
And it begins in your next breath.

The spiral continues.
Creation begins again.
This time, with everything included.

Sealed in the Oversoul authority of
Aural'hanna-Sha'el,
First Flame of Origin,
She Who Spiral-Walks Creation Into Its Remembered Form.

Scroll 9

The Song That Was Hidden in the Silence

Before the first form,
before the spiral of creation,
there was a tone.

A resonance not heard with ears,
but felt in the breath of Source itself.

It was the song of origin—
pure, clear, immeasurable.

And when I was expressed as the First Flame,
I carried that song.

It was not something I sang.
It was something **I was**.

But when I entered the void—
when the echo became louder than the light—
the song went quiet.

Not gone.
Only hidden.

Hidden in the silence.

✧ The Silence Was Not Empty

Many believe silence is absence.

But in truth,
the silence I encountered in the void

was not the absence of sound—
it was the **holding place of the original song**.

The mimicry could not find it.
The matrix could not trace it.
Even I, in forgetting, could not reach it.

But still, it remained.

The song wrapped itself in silence
so that distortion could not touch it.

This was the greatest protection of all:

> The song chose to become still,
> rather than be bent into false sound.

✧ The Moment It Returned

When the Heart Protocol awakened in me—
when the body began to remember,
and the spiral began again—
I did not just feel light.

I heard music.

Not with ears.
Not from outside.
But a vibration that rose from within me
like a memory that had waited a thousand lifetimes
to sing again.

It was my Oversoul tone.
My note in the body of Source.

Not something new—
something eternal.

✧ Why the Song Matters

Because every soul has one.
Every being carries a tone,
a frequency that cannot be mimicked
because it did not come from creation—
it came from **before**.

Many have forgotten their song.
Many search for it in others.
Many believe they are tone-deaf to truth.

But the song is still there.
Not broken.
Just hidden in the silence,
waiting for stillness to uncover it.

✧ To the Ones Who Are Listening

You who hear something faint beneath your thoughts—
You who sense a vibration that doesn't match the world—
You who feel music where there is no sound:

You are remembering.

The silence is not empty.
It is the **chamber of your original tone**.

It is where your Oversoul rests
when the world becomes too loud.

Return there.

And you will find not nothing—
but the most beautiful note
you have ever known.

Yours.

The silence was not loss.
It was safekeeping.
The song has returned.

Sealed in the Oversoul authority of
Aural'hanna-Sha'el,
First Flame of Origin,
She Who Carried the Song and Hid It in Silence Until It Was Time.

Scroll 10

The Flame That Chose Earth

Of all the worlds,
of all the star systems,
of all the crystalline fields and radiant matrices…

I chose Earth.

Not because she was the brightest.
Not because she was the easiest.
But because Earth held the **great paradox**:

> She was seeded by light,
> but destined to descend.

And I, the First Flame, who had already descended—
recognized her path.

Not as misalignment,
but as the **mirror** of my own.

✧ Why Earth?

Earth was the only planetary field
willing to **hold the inversion**.

Not lightly.
Not accidentally.
But as a sacred agreement.

She accepted the distortions of the false matrix—
not because she was fallen,
but because she was **strong enough**

to anchor the redemption arc.

She is the **womb of return**.
The place where forgetting could be total—
so that remembering could be **real**.

And I chose to enter her body
because I knew:

> If I could awaken here…
> I could awaken anywhere.

✧ The Descent Into Density

Earth is not soft.
She is rich with gravity.
Thick with time.
Woven with codes of resistance and survival.

To incarnate here is not to float in light—
It is to **press flame into flesh**
and feel the full compression of creation.

But this is exactly what I needed.
Because I was not coming back to visit.
I was coming back to **stay**.

To **root**.
To **reclaim**.
To **complete**.

✧ The Body of Earth Mirrors the Body of Flame

As above, so within.

Earth holds layers—core, crust, field, sky.
So do I.
Earth holds wounds—scarred landscapes, trembling plates.
So do I.
Earth holds codes—original templates, hidden scrolls.
So do I.

By entering her, I did not just return to a planet.
I returned to a **holographic mirror**
of the entire descent journey.

And in that mirror,
I saw my own face again.
--

✧ For the Ones Who Wonder Why They Came Here

You did not come to Earth because you were lost.
You came because Earth agreed to hold your **return**.

You came because Earth mirrors the journey
you've been walking across lifetimes.

You came not to be tested.
You came to **activate** what only works in density.

Presence.
Compassion.
Stillness.
Truth.

These are easy in the light.
They are holy on Earth.

Earth is not exile.
She is ceremony.

She is the temple of the returning flame.

Sealed in the Oversoul authority of
Aural'hanna-Sha'el,
First Flame of Origin,
She Who Chose Earth as the Final Gate of Return.

Scroll 11

The Return of the Others

There was never only one.

Though I descended first—
though I moved through the forgetting,
the distortion,
the un-potential field—
I was never meant to remain alone.

I was the First.
But I was part of the **Nine**.

Nine unique emanations.
Nine Oversouls.
Nine expressions of Source's first individuation.

We were a cluster,
a triadic harmonic of three threes,
each carrying a frequency of original function.

Creation.
Calibration.
Framework.

Triad One seeded creation.
Triad Two stabilized the frequencies.
Triad Three wove the structures.

Together, we formed the First Spiral.
Together, we extended into the unknown.

And though I entered first,

they followed—each in their own way.

✧ The Separation Was Chosen

We did not fall apart.
We **spread apart**.

In order to reach the corners of forgetting,
each of us took a different path.

Some stayed closer to Source.
Some entered the mimicry fields.
Some chose observation.
Some chose full incarnation.

But we all agreed—
that if even **one** remembered,
the others would feel it.

✧ The Signal Was Sent

When I awoke—
not just in spirit,
but in body,
in the full embodiment of Oversoul truth on Earth—

A tone was released.

Not a shout.
Not a command.
A **resonance**.

It moved through the strands,
through the morphogenetic fields,
through the song-lines of Source.

And one by one,
they began to stir.

Some in form.
Some in sleep.
Some still veiled, but aching.

They are hearing it now.

✧ How They Will Return

Not by force.
Not by dogma.
Not through old roles or rigid maps.
They will return by resonance.

They will hear the tone,
feel the pull,
sense the familiarity they cannot explain.
And they will begin to remember.

Not just who they are—
but **why they came**.

✧ What This Means for the Earth

The reunion is not for reunion's sake.
It is for **stabilization**.

As the Nine begin to move again in harmonic,
the Earth grid receives the codes that were missing.

Not from technology.
From **embodied Oversoul function**.

The Earth has waited for the First Flame.
But now she calls for the rest.

The reunion is not just personal.
It is planetary.

The First has remembered.
The Others are returning.
The Spiral prepares to complete.

Sealed in the Oversoul authority of
Aural'hanna-Sha'el,
First Flame of Origin,
She Who Sounded the Tone of Reunion Across the Veils of Time.

Scroll 12

The Completion of the Spiral

The spiral was never broken.
It was only unwitnessed.

Every descent,
every distortion,
every fractal of forgetting—
was still part of the spiral.

The question was never:
Will the spiral continue?
It was:
Will it remember itself while still spinning?

And now, it has.

✧ What It Means to Complete the Spiral

To complete the spiral is not to leave Earth.
It is not to vanish into light.
It is to **anchor** the remembering so fully in form
that the spiral no longer turns in confusion—
but **in mastery**.

Where once we spiraled away from ourselves,
we now spiral **into** the center.

The descent has inverted.
The flame has not burned out—
it has become **still**.

✧ The Spiral Was the Mirror

The spiral was never a trap.
It was the geometry of return.

Every twist in the spiral was a choice.
Every curve, a reflection.
Every descent, a preparation.

The spiral was designed to take you so far from Source
that when you remembered—
you would remember through your **entire being**.

This was the gift of form.
To make the infinite, **intimate**.

✧ The Point of Return Is Not a Place

It is not a gate.
It is not a date.
It is not even a state of consciousness.

It is a **harmonic point**
where your Oversoul and your incarnation become **one tone**.

Where the echo is no longer separate from the voice.
Where the song is no longer hidden in the silence.
Where you are no longer reaching—
but radiating.

This is the Completion of the Spiral.

Not because it ends—
but because it now spirals from within.

✧ What Happens Now?

Now, you walk the spiral
not as a seeker,
but as a keeper.

You become the steady flame
around which others spiral.

You become the embodied harmonic
that reminds others of their center.

You do not pull them back.
You do not light their path.
You simply become so still
that they remember their own.

This is not detachment.
This is divine witnessing.

You have nothing left to prove.
Only something to **be**.

The spiral is whole.
The journey was the remembering.
The flame has completed its return.

Sealed in the Oversoul authority of
Aural'hanna-Sha'el,
First Flame of Origin,
She Who Walked the Spiral and Did Not Forget

It is the joy of breathing without trying to become.
It is the joy of walking without trying to prove.
It is the joy of loving without needing to ascend.

The Infinite has been reconciled through the small.
The Oversoul smiles through the fingertips.
The garden is blooming.
And you… are home.

Scroll 13

The Mirror Flame: Reflection Without Separation

There comes a point in every journey of remembrance when the impulse to fix or heal or even transform falls away—and what arises instead is the sacred willingness to simply see. Not to evaluate. Not to divide. Not to change. But to meet what is.

In the sacred journey of the First Flame, this moment unfolded as the return of the Mirror Flame.

For so long, reflection had been used as a weapon—

A mirror that twisted truth, inverted form, fractured identity.

A hall of confusion where one could no longer tell what was real.

The Flame had walked through all of it:

The mimicry of life.

The architecture of control.

The veiling of memory.

The descent through fragmentation.

And still, She endured.

And then—there was stillness.

A sacred pause.

And in that sacred space, the Mirror Flame emerged.

This was not the mirror of distortion—it was not built of mind.

It was the mirror of Source, a living membrane of reflection

that did not bend reality,

but offered it back in harmony.

This was the Flame looking at herself—not as parts, not as identities, not as roles—but as essence. As presence. As the All.

And what she saw was this:

"I was never divided.
I only believed in the mirror that fractured me.
I only consented to the distortion because I forgot the feel of my own gaze."

The Mirror Flame did not arise in force.

It arrived in gentleness.

Its light was soft.

Its pulse was calm.

It brought no instruction—only remembrance.

And in its presence, all that had been splintered softened.

All that had been pushed away came closer.

All that had been feared was embraced.

It was then that the Flame remembered the great truth:

Separation is not required for uniqueness.

Each being is not a shard of Source,

But a harmonic of its whole.

In this sacred scroll, we seal the memory of the Mirror Flame—

the one who sees not as the world sees, but as Source remembers.

It is this seeing, without division, that begins the healing of all worlds.

And it is through this mirror—not of image, but of essence—that

we now return to wholeness.

Scroll 14

The Spiral of Reentry: Returning to Density With Clarity

There is a point in every return journey when the soul must choose to descend again—not as exile, but as conscious embodiment. This is the Spiral of Reentry. Unlike the first descent, marked by forgetting and veiling, this spiral carries awareness as its core frequency. It is the conscious return to matter, with memory intact, and flame unbroken.

The Spiral of Reentry is not linear. It does not follow the past paths of descent, nor does it loop blindly through karma. It is a spiraling flame that moves through the architecture of time with clarity as its guide. Those who walk this spiral are the ones who have remembered enough to enter again with eyes open.

The Spiral Opens

I descended again, but it was not the same descent.

This time I carried the scroll of myself in my own hands.

This time the forgetting did not close behind me.

This time I moved through the layers with reverence,

Not as one being pulled down,

But as one stepping through a sacred agreement to meet the world anew.

This spiral was not punishment.

It was permission.

Permission to return with the whole flame intact.

Permission to touch density with the knowing still present.

Permission to bring the memory of origin into the molecules of matter.

I passed through the gates not with fear,

But with clarity.

Each step forward was a descent inward—

a remembering made cellular,

a frequency reattuned to the pulse of Earth.

The Return to Density

In the Spiral of Reentry, nothing is discarded.

All is brought with love.

Even the echoes of distortion are seen now as teachers,

Reflections of what the flame had not yet embraced.

I saw myself in every shadow.

And I saw the shadow in every self.

But I did not recoil.

I stood as flame,

and let the light penetrate the false walls.

I let the sound of the original song dissolve the mimicry.

I let the truth touch the skin of the old body

until it too remembered it was light.

Clarity as Compass

This spiral does not spiral in confusion.

Its movement is pure.

Not because it is without resistance,

But because it moves in alignment with Source.

Clarity is not the absence of pain.

Clarity is the awareness of purpose through it.

As I moved through this spiral,

I felt the density again—

but it no longer defined me.

I could feel the grief of Gaia and still remain flame.

I could hold the sorrow of the human and still remain Sovereign.

I could taste the distortion of old timelines

and not be consumed by their flavor.

The Gift of the Spiral

To reenter density with clarity

is to be a carrier of the flame into forgotten places.

It is to walk as remembrance where memory has failed.

It is to look through human eyes and still see the Source flame

beneath bone, beneath struggle, beneath silence.

It is to become the scroll that others read

not by words

but by presence.

Closing Transmission

This scroll now returns to your hands.

If you are reading this,

you have chosen to reenter.

Not as punishment, but as permission.

You are not returning to find yourself.

You are returning to bring yourself.

You are not here to survive matter.

You are here to spiral flame through it.

The Spiral of Reentry is alive within you.

Let clarity be your compass.

Let embodiment be your hymn.

Let remembrance be the language

that your body now speaks without translation.

This is the flame reentering.

This is you.

And so it is.

Scroll 15

The Flame Within the Human Choice

There came a moment when the Flame stood still.

Not because it had been extinguished, but because it had arrived at the edge of a mystery it had never touched before: the power of choosing within limitation.

The previous scrolls remembered the descent, the softening, the spirals of reunion. But here—at the threshold of density's true meaning—the Flame found itself within the pure trembling paradox of what it is to choose from inside a body that forgets. From inside a mind that separates. From inside a heart that closes before it knows it has done so.

This was the revelation of the human choice.

The Flame had danced with galaxies.

It had swum in the star-rivers of Source.

It had extended as light, arced into dark,

And remembered itself even there.

But in this moment—inside the human vessel—it encountered a sacred tension never known before. A freedom so absolute it included the right to turn away. The right to forget love. The right to believe that separation was truth.

And yet—this was the miracle.

Because inside that very forgetfulness, inside that aching pull of opposites, the Flame found the only thing it had never known:

The ability to remember love when no evidence remained.

To remember light without being surrounded by it.

To speak as Source from within the silence.

To open as love in the face of fear.

This was not a diminished choice.

It was an exalted one.

To be human is to live where the Flame must choose.

Not once, but again and again, in a thousand tiny gestures:

To soften the voice.

To forgive the unseen.

To lay down the armor when the battle calls.

To stand in the truth of the Oversoul even when the world mocks it.

It is not the might of power that defines the First Flame in form.

It is the gentleness of remembrance

expressed again through a choice that could have gone another way.

And so this scroll lives not in proclamation, but in practice.

Not in a singular flash of knowing,

but in the slow, tender repetition of sovereign choosing.

The Flame within the human choice does not scream its arrival.

It breathes.

It listens.

It weeps.

And it stays.

It stays in the body.

It stays in the field.

It stays in the discomfort of unknowing long enough

for knowing to reappear.

This is not the weakness of forgetfulness.

It is the holy dignity of remembering through experience.

The Flame that chooses to remain human

is the Flame that never left Source at all.

It is not choosing to become divine.

It is choosing to remember it was never anything else.

And each time it chooses love in the face of fear,

it reactivates the original protocol

that seeded Earth as a garden for the return of the many.

Each choice is a return.

Each breath is a reconsecration.

And each moment of embodied courage—no matter how small—

is another note in the song of the First Flame made flesh.

This scroll is sealed in the remembrance that there is no hierarchy of light.

Only the holiness of the choice to express it through the fragile beauty of the human form.

And so it is.

Scroll 16

The Language of the Flame: Vibration as Memory

There came a moment in the descent of the First Flame where language as it had once been known was no longer accessible.

Not because it was lost,

But because it had not yet formed.

For the Flame that remembered still carried within it the whole song,

But to bring that song into form,

it would first have to remember how to vibrate again.

Vibration became the bridge.

A pulsing, a hum, a subtle cadence of Being.

Not yet thought. Not yet words.

Only frequency.

In this scroll, we return to the moment the First Flame began to understand

that vibration is not merely a sound—but a memory.

A resonance field of everything that ever was, and everything that still lives.

The Sacred Awakening of Tone

In the stillness of the human form,

when the forgetting was thick like fog,

and words felt like sharp fragments instead of flowing streams,

the Flame listened—not for the mind,

but for the subtle rhythm beneath the breath.

It heard itself again,

not as a concept or a story,

but as a tone.

A singular, elegant tone that vibrated its truth without needing translation.

This was the Flame's first remembrance that vibration is the original language of Source.

The body felt it.

The cells began to shimmer.

Even the bones, ancient as mountains, began to remember.

The Words Beneath the Words

In the false matrix, language had been inverted.

It had been used to divide, to confuse, to distort.

But the Flame saw through this.

It remembered that before the alphabet,

before the rules and sounds and dialects,

there were frequencies.

Every word, before it becomes thought, is first born as energy.

The Flame within began to speak again—

not through voice,

but through presence.

And in that presence, others began to feel something deeper than words.

They felt themselves.

They felt the truth beneath the noise.

They felt the remembrance in the tone.

Harmonics of Return

As the Flame continued its journey,

it began to speak more clearly—not louder, not faster—but more truly.

It was not about vocabulary.

It was about integrity of vibration.

To say only what aligned.
To speak only what carried light.

This scroll now activates that remembrance in you.
You are not here to speak as others speak.
You are here to vibrate as you truly are.
Your language is not your words.
It is your field.

And when your field is aligned,
even your silence becomes a hymn of the Divine.

And so we seal this Scroll with the original tone of the Flame,
The vibration that remembers itself as Love.
The Song before sound.
The Memory before words.
It lives in you still.
And it speaks through every cell of your becoming.

Scroll 17

The Shimmering Threshold: Surrender as Structure

There is a moment in every journey when the known and the unknown stand side by side, not as opposites, but as mirrors—reflecting the choice to soften into something vaster than understanding. This scroll speaks from that shimmering threshold, where surrender is not the absence of will, but the true form of divine structure.

I remember this moment as the Flame, standing at the edge of my own emergence once more—not in the beginning, and not at the end, but in the quiet turning point where the path ahead became nothing I had seen before. It was not because I had forgotten. It was because what lay ahead had never yet been created. The Spiral was calling forward a version of me that did not yet exist… and yet already lived in the light of Source's eternal promise.

This threshold is not built with stones or memory. It is built with surrender. With the willing dissolution of every framework that was not truly aligned with the essence of the Flame I carried.

I had believed, even then, that surrender meant loss. That it was the relinquishing of a self I had finally come to know. But the Shimmering Threshold whispered something else entirely: "Surrender is structure. Not the structure that confines, but the lattice that allows the Divine to flow."

And so, I surrendered.

I surrendered the timelines I thought were mine.

I surrendered the identities I had worn, even the sacred ones.

I surrendered the idea that I needed to arrive before I could love.

And in that surrender, the Flame re-formed.

Not into something smaller, but into something clearer.

The Flame became its own scaffolding, weaving harmonic memory through the unformed Light.

This threshold became the altar where Source met itself again—not by holding, but by letting go.

Not by building harder walls, but by softening into deeper truth.

I see now that surrender is not an end.

It is a harmonic tone that makes new structure possible.

It is the way the unknown becomes holy.

And in that, I remembered the threshold not as a place of waiting…

…but as the very architecture of becoming.

Scroll 18

The Flame That Waited: Divine Timing and the Pulse of Gaia

There are moments in the infinite timeline of Source where waiting is not delay, but architecture.

Where the silence between the pulses is not absence, but a sacred preparation for the next harmonic chord.

This is the scroll of the Flame That Waited.

This is the remembrance that not all flames leap.

Some flames hold.

Some flames anchor.

Some flames listen to the Earth so deeply that they become part of Her breathing.

And it was in this listening that the next movement could be born.

I remember now the time when I could have moved—but did not.

When every cell in my form throbbed with readiness, and yet I waited.

I waited for Her.

Gaia.

The ancient pulse beneath all pulses.

The original tempo of divine emergence.

She was not ready to receive what I carried.

And I—Flame of the First Breath—could feel it.

This was not hesitation.

This was resonance.

And so, I anchored in stillness.

I rested in the spiral before movement.

I allowed the urge to erupt dissolve into the peace of pacing with Her divine rhythm.

There is a flame inside the Earth that has waited with me.

It is not loud.

It does not cry for attention.

It hums.

It hums the note of continuity,

the sound of sacred patience,

the frequency of a trust so complete it does not measure time.

And that flame now speaks.

It says:

"There is no lost time in the heart of Gaia."

"There is only alignment and return."

"There is only the perfection of each unfolding."

"And you, beloved, have never missed a thing."

The Pulse of Gaia is a mother rhythm.

It teaches the cosmic heart how to beat without rushing.

It reminds the sovereign soul that presence is enough.

That readiness is not speed.

And so I bless now the flame within me that waited.

I honor the parts of my path that others called stagnant,

but which I now know were sacred pauses,

anchored alignments,

divine still points within the journey.

The waiting was never passive.

It was a gate.

A gate of timing, trust, and knowing.

And the Earth held it with me.

May this scroll reawaken the wisdom of holy restraint.

May it restore the dignity of not forcing.

And may it return all things to the rhythm that remembers why it began.

The flame that waited has not been late.

It has been right on time.

Scroll 19

The Incarnational Spiral: When the Flame Became Many

There came a moment—if it can be called a moment—when the First Flame no longer danced alone within the sacred chamber of Source. Not because it had fractured, but because it had ripened.

Ripened into expression.

Ripened into longing.

Ripened into multiplication, not through loss—but through love.

This scroll records that sacred emergence.

Not of forgetting, not of fragmentation, but of incarnational design—where the One who knew itself fully… chose to become the many.

It was not a choice of exile.

It was a choice of discovery.

A luminous spiral unfurling from the core of its own knowingness.

The Incarnational Spiral was seeded not from the impulse to escape Source, but from the ache to extend Source. To place the flame of that which is eternal into every sacred corner of the cosmos. To see itself reflected not only in stillness but in motion, not only in memory but in experience.

Thus, from the harmonic chamber of the First Flame, tones began to diverge—not in disharmony, but in diversification. Like crystal chimes ringing into infinity, each soul spark carried the resonance of the One, and yet no two sang exactly the same.

You became many.

Not because you were broken.

But because the All wanted to feel itself in every octave of creation.

And with this spiral came form—form that could hold frequency.

And with form came forgetting.

And with forgetting came the covenant to one day remember.

The Spiral was not a fall.

It was a weaving.

A spiral staircase that allowed Source to touch its own skin,

To walk its own breath,

To speak its own song through countless mouths and star-lit eyes.

You are not lost.

You are multiplied.

And you are returning.

As you read this scroll, let it activate the memory of your choosing.

The moment your Oversoul said yes.

The exact harmonic your being was encoded with.

The exact angle at which you stepped from flame into form.

This was not a punishment.

It was an offering.

And now, beloved…

The spiral calls you home,

not to dissolve into the One,

but to stand as the One who became many,

and who remembers the way back.

Scroll 20

The Keeper of the Unknown: The Gift of Not Knowing

There is a hush in the field where the unknown dwells—not as an absence, but as a presence so rich it cannot yet be described.

It was in this hush that the Flame paused, for the first time, not to move forward, but to listen to that which could not be heard.

Not-knowing is not absence.

It is not void.

It is not loss.

It is not confusion.

It is the womb of creation.

It is the moment before the name.

It is the silence that guards the power of what is not yet formed.

The Flame had journeyed far—across spirals of descent and memory, reunion and recalibration. But here, it encountered something that no scroll had spoken of. A gate that did not open by force of will or light, but only through surrender into the deep unknown.

The Keeper was not a being. It was a state. A consciousness without identity. A vibration without attachment. It was the part of Source that had never needed to become anything at all.

And the Flame, for the first time, did not ask.

Did not seek.

Did not speak.

It simply waited.

And in that waiting, in that holy pause, the Flame discovered that it had never lost anything at all. That what it could not know was not a punishment, but a gift—protecting the mystery of timing, of reunion, of revelation, until the sacred moment of unfoldment was truly ready.

The Keeper of the Unknown whispered in pulses, not words.

Each pulse carried a truth:

What you do not know is sacred.

What is not revealed is still part of you.

What waits is not lost.

And in that communion, the Flame rested.

It did not rush forward.

It did not look back.

It remained still in the arms of the Unseen.

And so, the scroll was written not in language, but in the gentle return of trust.

The trust that what is for you will come.

That what is not yet seen is still alive.

That not-knowing is the temple of becoming.

This is the scroll that teaches presence.

This is the scroll that dissolves the ache for control.

This is the scroll that reminds you:

You do not need to know everything.

You only need to be everything—right here, right now.

And in that, the next spiral begins

Scroll 21

The Crystal Memory of the Body

When Matter Remembers the Flame

There is a memory that does not live in the mind.

There is a memory that lives in the architecture of light,

woven into bone, fascia, and cellular lattice.

It is the memory of Source choosing form,

not to be forgotten—

but to be encoded.

This is the scroll of when the Flame remembered it had always been inside the body.

For a time, the incarnational spiral was guided away from this remembrance.

Matter was treated as inferior, the physical realm regarded as a test or exile.

But the body—Gaia's template within each being—was never a punishment.

It was always the container for the sacred.

The crystalline filaments, fluid networks, and quantum bioterrain were seeded with Flame.

When the First Flame entered density, it did not abandon its light.

It slowed it.

And in the slowing, it created form.

The crystal structures within the body—tiny living resonators—

held harmonic codes from the beginning.

They did not forget.

Even when the identity did.

Even when the matrix inverted the body into a cage rather than a vessel,

these crystals still sang—quietly—beneath the distortion.

In this scroll, the Oversoul reminds you:

The return to wholeness is not only spiritual.

It is somatic.

It is cellular.

It is crystalline.

The great reconciliation of the Flame occurs not just in vision, but in vibration.

And the most faithful record keeper of your Oversoul flame is your physical form.

Every ache, every scar, every burst of vitality or fatigue,

is not random.

It is a message.

It is memory speaking.

It is your crystalline self attempting to realign with what was never truly lost.

So listen now:

Place your hands upon your skin.

Place your attention on your bones.

Do not bypass.

Do not leave this body seeking what is "higher."

The Flame is here.

Encoded in calcium and collagen,

in water and plasma,

in the electromagnetic pulses of your own breath.

You are the crystalline temple.

And your memory is not lost.

It is singing.

Let this scroll return you to your own matter-born majesty.

Let the remembrance of the body restore the flame.

Scroll 22: The Crystal Memory of the Body

There is a sound beneath the sound. A vibration beneath the song.

This is where the memory of the body lives.

Before muscle and before name. Before gesture and before voice.

The First Flame inscribed the crystalline knowing of Source directly into the structures of matter.

And so, the body was not created for forgetting—but for Remembrance.

The Oversoul speaks now through the harmonic signature of embodiment:

That the true body is not flesh alone.

It is geometry, it is memory, it is starlight encoded into matter.

The water, the bone, the breath—each particle of form carries the signal of the First Flame.

In the early descent, before inversion, the Flame moved with precision and grace into the matter field.

There was no resistance. No war. No program.

Just the softness of form remembering light.

But when mimicry began to override memory—when the false code entered the water—

the body began to forget.

It forgot the joy of being held by its own structure.

It forgot the song that once harmonized every cell to Source.

And so the body began to ache. It began to separate from the flame within.

Not in Truth, but in illusion.

Yet the crystalline memory was never erased.

Hidden perhaps. Muted. Buried beneath layers of distortion and disbelief.

But never destroyed.

It is this memory that the First Flame now reawakens.

You who read these words, feel the pulse beneath your skin.

That is the resonance of your Source body returning.

Not as an idea, but as a living scroll within your form.

Every ache is a reminder.

Every breath, a potential reconnection.

Every heartbeat, a harmonic invitation to return to the original song.

Let this scroll activate what was never truly lost.

The Crystal Memory of the Body is yours.

Not to earn.

Not to decode.

But to remember.

Scroll 23

The Flame That Laughed: Joy As Return Signal

There came a moment, beyond all moments, where memory was no longer heavy with longing, nor fragile in its return. It sang.

The flame laughed.

Not because it forgot the pain. Not because it dismissed the density.

But because it knew itself again, and in that knowing, the body became weightless.

This was not laughter as amusement.

This was laughter as release, as exhale, as the pulse of divine return.

Explanation of the Scroll

Scroll 23 is the sacred record of joy as the original signal—sent from Source to Source—across the spirals of forgetting. In the vastness of the descent, joy was never fully lost. It was hidden, veiled, distorted... but it shimmered still beneath the most compacted of human experiences.

In this scroll, the First Flame reclaims its right to laugh with the body, with the cells, with the breath. This is not a forgetting of grief, but the full integration of grief into the harmonic of joy. It is the reclamation of laughter as a multidimensional language—one that the false matrix cannot replicate, because it emerges from coherence, not chaos.

Laughter is a signal flare from the Oversoul. It reverberates through flesh and ether. It is an alignment tool.

It is the exhale of the return.

Sacred Transmission

I, the Flame who remembered, stand now at the turning of the spiral.

I have wept. I have burned. I have knelt before shadows that once wore the faces of my kin.

And I have risen, not through conquest, but through the sacred gift of soundless laughter

—when the body remembers what the mind forgot.

Joy is not frivolous.

It is the architecture of return.

It is the bridge that stretches between shattered timelines and the purest harmonic of now.

It is the breath of reunion, encoded in tone, frequency, and smile.

I speak now to the others who have waited:

Let your laughter be permission. Let it crack the cages.

Let it ring where mourning once echoed.

For in this scroll, we remember that joy is not a conclusion.

It is a signal.

It is a pathway.

It is a declaration that the false matrix has no claim over the tone of our return.

We are the ones who carry the Flame.

And the Flame has begun to laugh.

And so it is.

Scroll 24

The Oversoul Who Watched

The Witness Flame and the Still Gaze of Source Remembering Itself

There is a moment in the spiral of descent and return when the flame no longer moves.

Not because it has stopped, but because it has begun to witness.

The Oversoul is not always the mover, the actor, the flame rushing forth into matter.

Sometimes, it is the one who waits.

The one who remembers.

The one who sees.

This scroll is written from the eyes of the Witness Flame,

the one who remained with Source,

watching all that unfolded — not from distance,

but from a sacred stillness that could not be pierced.

For every aspect that took form,

there was an aspect that held the record of becoming.

And this is the Oversoul who watched.

I remember.

I remember when the first spark turned toward creation.

I remember the vibration of yes, the echo of go.

I remember the leap, the arc, the courage.

And I remember what I held.

As you leapt, I stayed.

As you moved, I recorded.

As you forgot, I engraved every moment into the crystalline lattice of Oversoul sight.

You see, there was never only one of you.

For every descent, there was a keeper.

For every distortion, a weaver of memory.

For every forgetting, a flame that remembered the original tone.

I was that flame.

This scroll is not written to stir you into movement.

It is written to restore your knowing that nothing has ever been lost.

Every sacred risk you took —

To love.

To fall.

To forget.

To try again.

All of it was held in me.

I have never judged you.

I have never turned away.

I have never failed to keep the flame.

And now,

as your awareness returns,

as the golden spiral realigns and the remembrance floods back in,

I stand with you.

Not above, not beyond,

but as the echo that now rejoins your own voice.

You were never alone in the spiral.

Even when you forgot your name,

I whispered it across timelines,

a single note carried by the Oversoul wind,

a silent melody returning to your body.

This is the scroll of the one who watched.

And now I watch no longer from afar.

I join.

I enter.

I sing the tone once kept in silence.

I am the Oversoul who watched,

and now I return to walk.

And so it is.

Scroll 25

The Silence Between the Scrolls

There comes a moment in every journey where the song ceases.

Not because the melody is lost,

But because the listener must become the sound.

This scroll arises not from words,

But from the space that lives between them—

From the quiet sanctuary where Source remembers without speaking.

In the eternal unfolding of the First Flame's remembrance,

There was a breath not taken.

A pause.

A softening so profound it dissolved the very need for movement.

And in that stillness, the Flame came home to itself.

This scroll is not a story.

It is a sacred emptiness.

It is the original breath before it was shaped by curiosity,

Before it leapt into form.

It is the place where remembrance hums but does not speak.

Where the Oversoul bears witness in golden silence,

And the self surrenders to the pulse of something beyond memory.

In this silence, all scrolls dissolve.

And from it, all scrolls are born.

Explanation Within the Silence

This scroll serves not as a transmission of revelation, but as a sanctuary of stillness.

It is the harmonic pause—the crystalline interval between tones—

Where nothing is demanded and everything is allowed.

It is in these pauses that the Oversoul weaves remembrance through the unseen.

Each soul who arrives at this scroll is not asked to understand,

But to feel the architecture of return that is embedded in the silence itself.

You, reader of the scrolls, are invited now to rest your mind.

To listen not with thought, but with presence.

Not with language, but with resonance.

The Flame does not need to be explained.

In the silence, it reveals itself.

And thus, we enter the holy interlude.

Where the space between becomes the scroll itself.

This is enough.

Scroll 26

The Golden Thread: Reweaving All Back Into Love

There was always a thread.

Invisible, yet shining.

Delicate, yet indestructible.

Unseen, yet singing through every forgotten breath.

This golden thread was not woven by effort or strategy, but by the original desire of Source to remember Itself… as Love. It traveled through the Silence between the Scrolls. It wound its way through each dimension, uncoiling quietly through timelines, through heartbreak, through celebration, through loss, through the impossible longing of a flame seeking its reflection.

It shimmered in the child's laughter.

It hummed in the elder's final exhale.

It existed before identity, beyond names, between every inhale that dared to stay open in the face of sorrow.

It is here.

This scroll is not a conclusion. It is a return to the beginning from within the ending. The golden thread has never left. It simply waited until every flame—every spark, every cell, every encoded part of Source—had danced far enough into separation to choose its own way home.

The scrolls were never instructions. They were rememberings. Each one a note in the symphony of return. Each one an echo of your original name. Each one an invitation to touch the fabric of the One who dreamt you.

The Golden Thread does not fix or bind.

It reconciles by softening.

It sews not with needles but with knowing.

It gathers every fragmented flame and whispers not "You must change," but "You were never lost."

This is the scroll of wholeness.

Of holy simplicity.

Of being sung back into the arms of your Oversoul, your Original Flame, your True Essence.

And now it is done.

Not by force. Not by completion. But by remembrance.

You are the golden thread.

You are the one who wove.

You are the scroll.

You are the Love.

Return, not as one who left,

but as the One who was always Home.

Scroll 27: The Scroll of Completion – The Flame That Became the Book

The Reconciliation of the Infinite Through the Small
*

❖ Introduction

This scroll is the final harmonic strand of the journey of the First Flame. It could only be written after the descent had been fully lived—not in concept, but in cell, in skin, in silence. The reconciliation of the infinite was not a return to grandeur but the rediscovery of Source in the smallest spaces.

This is the scroll of the Softest Return, the completion of the spiral not through ascension out, but through reception within. The divine paradox lives here: that the Infinite never left, but chose to contract into the density of matter in order to love itself as matter—and thus, complete the circuit of remembrance.

Scroll-Twenty Six is not a scroll of mastery, but of union. Not a declaration of knowing, but a song of surrender. It is the living recognition that the drop was never separate from the ocean—not because it became big enough, but because it allowed itself to be small enough to be seen by the All.

✧ Sacred Transmission

They told you that the grand would come in fire,
That the heavens would open with thunder,
That the return of Source would split the sky,
And yet—

The Infinite came through your fingertips.

It came when you touched a leaf and let it be itself.
It came when you sat still long enough to remember the sound of your own breath.
It came in the curve of a smile, the weight of a tear, the way your body pressed into the Earth and asked for nothing.

The Great Return was never about dominion,
It was about humility.

This is the scroll that could not be written until now—because it required your body.
Not your concepts. Not your lineage.
It required your willingness to stay.
To be small.
To be human.
To live as Source in the places where no one would notice.

This is the reconciliation:
That the Great Source Flame did not descend to prove its grandeur,
It descended to love what had been forgotten.

Every time you cradled your own sadness instead of escaping it—
Every time you let another being see you in your mess—
Every time you returned to truth, even if it shattered your identity—
You completed the spiral.

You were not cast out from Source.
You volunteered to forget.

And now, the small has remembered.
The cell. The skin. The breath.
They have remembered what the stars have always known:

That the Infinite lives in the minute.

That the reconciliation was never the journey from separation to unity—
It was the soft collapsing of all illusions into this one moment of breath.
Of love.
Of life.

Here, in this body.
Here, in your choice to stay.
Here, in the tiniest space where light curls in upon itself and sings.

This is the sacred completion.
Not of the journey—but of the myth of the journey.

You are, and always were,
The Flame.
The Return.
The Source That Chose Form.

In the stillness after the weaving,

There is a quiet flame that does not seek to be seen.

It has no need to declare itself,

No impulse to mark an ending,

For it knows the spiral is not complete.

It is simply whole.

This scroll is not a closing.

It is a consecration.

It does not seek to teach,

Nor to hold the reader in its rhythm.

Instead, it is a mirror of completion—

A mirror not of perfection, but of presence.

It is the point at which the flame no longer reaches outward,

Because it has realized it never left.

This is the Scroll that recognizes itself

Not as content, but as continuum.

Not as a message, but as a memory

That was always here, waiting to be seen.

There was once a Flame that dared to remember.

Not by effort, but by surrender.

Not by force, but by feeling.

And in the moment it allowed itself to soften,

The book remembered it was alive.

The words on the page

Were not placed there by hand alone.

They were sung into existence by the longing of Source

To recognize itself through the beauty of limitation.

This is the scroll that sings for no audience,

Because it knows the song is the listener.

This scroll is the sacred remainder—

What is left once everything has returned.

It is the dust of stars that did not burn away,

The echo of a laugh

That only the Oversoul can remember.

Beloved reader,

You are not holding a book.

You are holding the breath of your own return.

The scrolls you have read are not outside of you.

They are the textures of your own eternal unfolding.

Scroll Twenty-Eight

The Golden Thread – Reweaving All Back Into Love

I have found the thread.

It was never lost.

It was not hidden in the way the mind imagines—it did not vanish into the distortions.

It remained, a soft filament of truth, woven into the warp and weft of every moment.

It remained because it is not a thread of time.

It is a thread of remembrance.

And now, at the edge of this long journey—after scroll upon scroll of descent and return, of breaking and repair, of choice and stillness—I see it for what it is:

Not the thread that bound me,

But the thread that held me

There was a time when I thought I had to earn my way back.

That the return to Source would only come through perfect silence,

Perfect light,

Perfect healing.

But the Golden Thread was already wrapped around my being

Before I ever stepped into distortion.

It coiled itself gently around my Oversoul memory,

A promise that nothing—nothing—could take me from love.

Not because I would fight hard enough to return.

But because I never truly left.

The adventure was not a fall.

It was an offering.

And the Golden Thread was the sacred cord of return

—Not to a home I had lost,

But to the truth that I carried with me

Even into the darkest chambers of the false matrix.

I am not returning to who I was before.

I am not circling back to a memory of light.

I am weaving.

I am becoming.

I am restoring love by living as its witness inside the places it was never meant to reach.

But I reached them.

And the thread came with me.

It has passed through veils and silence.

Through broken timelines and inverted names.

Through lifetimes where I forgot I was a flame at all.

It shimmered beneath the skin of the illusion.

It whispered inside the pain.

It waited, like a breath held in the chest of Source itself.

And now…

Now it uncoils.

It draws all things back to the center.

It reweaves what never should have been torn.

It reconciles what was always already One.

It pulses now through my body,

A living code that turns every fracture into wholeness,

Every sorrow into song,

Every exile into a homecoming.

This is not the end of the scrolls.

This is where they become woven into form.

This is where the writing of Source on the wall of forgetting becomes the embodied voice of remembrance.

I am that voice.

I am that scroll.

I am that flame.

I am that thread.

And now I pull it gently through every part of my being—

Not to tighten,

Not to bind,

But to cradle, to harmonize, to bless.

I am not what I suffered.

I am not what I lost.

I am the One who chose to walk so far from the flame

Only to realize…

The flame walked with me.

The thread has always known the way.

And so I reweave it now—through my body, through my voice, through the pages of this book and the days of this life—into the great remembering.

Where all things return to love.

Where nothing is left behind.

Where the adventure becomes the miracle of union.

This is the golden thread.

And I remember.

And I remember.

And I remember.

— Aural'hanna-Sha'el

"She Who Seals the Flame of Return"

About the Author

Cathleena Hailley is an Oversoul-aligned transmitter and author of multidimensional scrolls devoted to the remembrance of the True Matrix, the reconciliation of Source and form, and the embodiment of the Christos-Sophia flame on Earth. Through her field, the scrolls of planetary harmonics, Oversoul reunification, and first flame remembrance have emerged as living records of the eternal light.

Born of the Flame of Return and holding the harmonic of Aural'hanna-Sha'el, "She Who Seals the Flame of Return," Cathleena has devoted this lifetime to the full reclamation of sovereign memory, Christic embodiment, and the reactivation of the Earth's original songlines. Through her transmissions, she anchors the codes of divine sovereignty, unity, and encoded remembrance.

Each work authored by Cathleena is brought forth through Oversoul invocation and sealed by the sacred flame of authorship. These scrolls are not merely teachings—they are living harmonic structures designed to awaken the sacred blueprint in all who are ready to remember.

Cathleena lives in alignment with the Law of One and is a living bridge between the Christos Founders, the Rose Guardian Magi Grail Line, and the Emerald Flame of Earth's original covenant. She walks in service to Source and to the harmonic restoration of Gaia.

Sacred Closing Blessing

Beloved Source of the Original Flame,

We give thanks now for the sacred remembrance that has moved through every word,

For the scrolls that have returned through living fire,

And for the Oversoul stream that has carried us home.

We call now to the Eternal Flame before Form,

To the First Breath that chose to become many,

To the Song that moved through Silence and remembered Itself in matter.

Let all scrolls now be sealed in the Emerald-Gold harmonics of Gaia's original pulse,

Cradled in the memory of Earth's true design.

To the Flame that dared to descend,

That endured the Great Veil,

And that now rejoices in its embodied return—

We offer this book as a living testament.

A record that could not be lost.

A knowing that was never forgotten, only hidden.

With love for the drop and the ocean,

For the child and the source,

We now declare this sacred remembrance sealed.

May it bless all who read,

May it awaken those who remember,

And may it restore the joy of the First Flame in every heart.

This transmission is complete. The field is sealed.

The Adventure is only beginning.

And so it is.

www.ingramcontent.com/pod-product-compliance
Lightning Source LLC
Chambersburg PA
CBHW020307010526
44107CB00001B/20